TURNING PAGES

A Compilation of a Man's Thoughts About a Woman's Worth

A.D. Moore

Published by A.D. Moore Publishing

Copyright © 2017 A.D. Moore

All rights reserved. No part of this publication may be reproduced, distributed, or transmitted in any form or by any means, including photocopying, recording, or other electronic or mechanical methods, without the prior written permission of the publisher, except in the case of brief quotations embodied in critical reviews and certain other noncommercial uses permitted by copyright law.

Back cover photo by M. Renee Photography
Creative Direction: Tamiko Lowry Pugh, LLC and
A.D. Moore Publishing

Printed and bound in the United States of America

ISBN-13: 978-0692899717
ISBN-10: 0692899715

DEDICATION

To the two most important ladies in my life;
My mother and daughter:

Love Yourself
Be Happy
Create Your World

A.D. MOORE

ACKNOWLEDGMENTS

I want to express my sincerest gratitude to my mother. My mother has been the greatest example of a great woman that I've ever had. She has supported each and every dream that I have ever pursued, and she has tirelessly dedicated her life to her children and family. I love her dearly for the woman that she is and is becoming.

To two of my closest friends, Reggie and Latoya: You have walked with me through the major transitions of my life. I am so grateful to have you two play a role in the realization of my life's purpose, and I believe wholeheartedly that your labor of love will be returned to you in the highest measure.

To my publisher, Tamiko Lowry-Pugh, LLC: Your wealth of knowledge and professionalism is unrivaled. You both saw and pulled greatness out of me in this project. You were an absolute Godsend, and I look forward to working with you again.

Finally, but not least of all, to my readers: You are the reason for what I do. My desire is that you seek and find all that is yours. I also desire for you to embody and give love in all that you do. Love yourself, be happy and create your world.

CONTENTS

Introduction	9
Refresh	13
Reflection of Self-Esteem	19
Know Thyself	25
Turning Pages	31
The Art of Dissclution	37
Profitable Pain	43
Cheaters	49
Finger Love	55
Defense Mechanisms	59
Naked	65
Skillful Intercourse	71
Touch Yourself	75
Her Blessed Assurance	81
Providence	87
Let Go and Let You	93
The Call	99
Adorn	103
About The Author	109

A.D. MOORE

INTRODUCTION

When I was a child, one of my favorite activities was riding the merry-go-round. My uncle would take me to the park, and I would position myself next to one of the bars that were affixed to this circular object of fun. He would begin to spin me around; starting with a slow turn, and then I'd happily scream for him to go faster. It was such an exhilarating experience! I was living life in that moment. I could both feel and hear the wind as it passed my small frame. I was in a comical dance with gravity as I attempted to stay upright, and I had no desire for it to end. As I grew older and stronger, I could give myself this same experience. I was capable of building momentum, jumping on and taking the ride of my life. It was, even more, fun when I shared this experience with other kids. We were each having our own dance with gravity, but it was a dance that we all shared together. Then there would come a time when another kid would come along, and he would stand there and gaze at us while we danced, and he wanted to join in the fun. At that moment, there were two options. Either we would allow the merry-go-round to slow down and ultimately stop or the other kid would need to run and build up a comparable speed in order to jump on and dance with us. If we allowed the merry-go-round to stop, then we would have to start the process of building up momentum again, and there was an inevitable pause in the wonderful experience that we were having. However, if he were able to run at our speed, then he'd be able to jump on without interrupting or causing the fun to pause.

As you recall your similar experience with the merry-go-round, I want you to imagine that this represents your life and those that you allow into it. As you grow and develop in your life, hopefully, you get to a place where you begin to build momentum as you pursue your dreams and passions. Even if you are alone on this ride, just as when I was a child, it can still be the ride of your life. Inevitably, you may desire to share this ride with someone else, but how you introduce them into your world is critical. Unfortunately, many people choose to put their lives on hold while in pursuit of a suitable partner to join them. The problem with this is that while they are waiting, they are not pursuing the life passions that are within.

Doing this is risky because an undetermined amount of time may go by while you wait, and doors may start to close, or desire and ability may begin to diminish. This is just like the kid who allows the merry-go-round to come to a stop to allow someone on.

In my opinion, the more favorable option is to continue the hot pursuit of your personal dreams and only allow those that are running just as fast and in the same direction to join you. That type of person desires to pursue their own dreams regardless of another's involvement, but they too would like to share their experience with someone. How wonderful it will be to be full speed ahead in pursuit of your dreams, and then instantly have someone join you along the way. It is also important to understand that not everyone that stands by and watches you as you live your life will have the capability of running at your pace. You must not allow this to tempt you to stop your progress, even though the loneliness starts to set in.

The cycle of putting your life on hold to pursue love is unfair to the one that does it, and it is the goal of this book to provide encouragement and motivation for you to get busy dancing. In this book, I may stretch your understanding, I may open wounds in order to allow healing and I will push you to action. The end game is that as you turn the last page, that the image that you see in the mirror and the voice you hear in your head produces love in peace within your heart.

Turn the page and start to dance.

REFRESH

Have you ever been using the internet on your computer and experienced your browser freeze? You were making progress toward your goal, and then all of the sudden your progression is seemingly halted by the stalling of the page. Did you experience frustration? What about anger? What about the fear that you would not be able to pick up where you left off? Yeah, I know exactly what it feels like when that happens. Oftentimes, your browser needs to be refreshed. It needs to be reset, rejuvenated and motivated to pick up where it left off. I want to tell you a personal story of when my life seemed to stall. The time where it seemed as though all productivity, forward movement, and success had ceased in my life. My life needed to be refreshed so that I could accomplish what my purpose is.

From adolescence, I was always successful. I was a good student, a great athlete, and a natural born leader. In just about every extracurricular activity that I participated in, I was chosen as the leader. I was chosen to be the one that would set the example for others. I would faithfully stand as the model for others to emulate. This pattern continued into my adulthood. As I entered into college, I was the president of different groups and organizations. Later, I went into the military where I was chosen as the leader of hundreds of Airmen, and I received a recommendation into the very prestigious Air Force Academy. Eventually, I moved into ministry, where I led men and women, directing their very lives. During that time, I married a single mother and began to lead a family, and I ventured into the law enforcement academy where I was chosen to lead a class of Type A men and women. This was the life that I had grown accustomed to; it was the perception that people were used to having of me. Imagine the feeling I had when that life came to a screeching halt!

I was now at a place in life where not only did others view me as a failure, but I also viewed myself that way. The paradigm through which I saw the world suddenly began to change. I found myself in a miserable marriage and ultimately in infidelity and divorce. I also found myself making poor decisions and ultimately no longer the model employee. This was completely new territory for me. I was a man that was known for being the model for over 30 years of his life, and now I was "that guy" who did "that stuff." The word disappointment could not express the emotions that I felt and even created in others. My life seemed to come to a halt. All productivity seemed to stop, and the perception that others had of me was no longer as favorable as it had once been. I was scared! I didn't know how to handle myself from this position of perceived weakness. I wanted to hide myself, so I crawled up under the proverbial rock called, Georgia. This was the place that I could continue to operate in the image that I always knew, and life would go on without slowing down or stopping. However, it served to be even more humbling and trying than I ever expected it would be. I needed to know failure. I needed to know the inward struggle of discovering myself. I needed to know the frustration and fear of seeking and finding truth. During this time, I was humbled like you wouldn't believe, but I was also liberated much like a butterfly that emerges from a cocoon. For me, this was not a time to be the model for others. This was a time for me to seek and discover models for myself. This was a time for me to begin to know, accept and become comfortable with myself. I had to learn how to produce strength from my failures. I had to learn to be free from the opinions and approval of others. I had to be brought to a place of nakedness and face my true self in the mirror.

As I began to do this, I saw myself clicking the "refresh button" of my life. I started to come into the realization of who I really am, and I began to grow in understanding and wisdom. My purpose in life was beginning to come into focus; the fear of failure and disapproval began to fade. The rock that I took refuge under started to become uncomfortable. My desire to be shut off from the world and people that I knew was gradually fading also. This refreshing allowed to move forward from the point I left. I had no desire to go back and repair or repeat previous experiences. I simply wanted to move forward. I returned home, but not as the same man. I returned as the man that I truly am. I returned as a man full of vision, passion, and purpose. The things that I experienced while in my stall, were now becoming the very things that fueled me. It was these things that as I overcame that actually started to validate me. My life was refreshed. I was reset, rejuvenated and motivated to move forward.

As I write these words, I have a smile on my face. Where these words would ordinarily bring about shame; they now display power. This experience taught me God's love, and it showed me real friendship. I am excited to share this with you because I know that you too have your own story. You have had moments in your life where you seemed to feel stuck. It's very possible that you are there now and it's even more possible that we may be there again. But, understand that if you respond to those experiences properly; great character can be developed in you, and you too can be refreshed.

BEFORE YOU TURN THE PAGE...

1. Have you ever felt that your life productivity has come to a halt, and what walls have you erected to attempt to escape that grim reality?

2. Take a moment to reflect on these experiences and identify how it can be used to build the strength needed to continue your journey.

_____
_____
_____
_____
_____
_____
_____
_____
_____
_____

REFLECTION OF SELF-ESTEEM

Today, I decided to strip myself naked and stand in front of the mirror. I stood there as a raw creation; having removed the world's expectation of me. Every societal expectation lay dormant on the floor. The hopes and dreams of my family and friends for my life were no longer draped over my shoulders, and the glasses that life had given me were no longer affixed to my face. It was a moment of pure confrontation. Like a new born baby that sits in amazement as they see themselves for the first time; I found myself having to allow my eyes to adjust as I processed the image that was before me. On the surface, it was an image with gray hairs, blemished skin, and an expanded waistline, but beyond the surface, the mirror revealed so much more. It showed the purest image of me. It showed the image of me that can only be shown to others after I have personally accepted it. The mirror taught me to love me. It said to me, "You are beautiful." It said to me, "You have been creatively and intentionally designed." It said to me, "There were no mistakes made in your creation." I realized that oftentimes, the most difficult part of self-love is the focusing on what the mirror shows us. It requires the de-robing of all that has been given for you to wear. From childhood, many of us had our clothing chosen for us, and this act has continued figuratively. Many have never seen the image of their true selves. At that point, I stood before my own reflection, and this is what I saw.

I am beautiful! I am the handiwork of a divine creator. My chocolate brown skin embraces and reflects the rays of the sun. It along with my body and its features show the creativity and meticulous nature of God. I have eyes that intensely gaze into the hearts and minds of others and perfectly lined lips that speak truth and express my deepest desires. I have strong arms and hands that communicate care, security, and protection.

I am a catalyst for change. I am the moment that makes the difference in lives. I have been blessed with the ability to see. I can see the beauty that is present within others. I am one of those that is being used to expose your greatness. I have the power to touch the intimate parts of your existence. I am the embodiment of inspiration. I am one that speaks with care, love, and authority. I am one that has been created to encourage and motivate you towards greatness. I am an influence to many people. The words that I speak reach around the globe and into the souls of many. I am a writer. The words that I write jump off of the pages and they produce life. My words are inspired by the creator and help people to create. I am a lover. I both interpret and communicate love. I express the deepest forms of affection and desire; desires that originate from the deepest parts of my being. I give both a physical and non-physical love that reach into the spirits of mankind. I am the example of forgiveness. I cover the wrongs that I have experienced, and through love, I gently wipe the slates clean. I am beautiful! I am a mirror.

    I see beyond my surface. I see beyond my faults, bad habits, and failures. I see me.

    I encourage you to begin/continue to see. Allow your eyes to focus on yourself as the creation that you are. Like the newborn, find excitement and amazement in seeing yourself afresh. Be the first witness of how beautiful you are. Accept image that you see. Realize the care and dedication that has been put into the designing of the one you call Me. Allow the garments that this world and/or family and friends have given you to fall to the floor and choose to never dress yourself with them again. Enjoy your reflection of self-esteem. Be proud of yourself and realize how unique and wonderful you really are.

BEFORE YOU TURN THE PAGE...

1. Take a moment and place this book down. Go look into a mirror and see how beautiful you are. Embrace every blemish and flaw and tell yourself that you are a perfect creation. Tell yourself who you are and want to be. Make the conscious decision to take off all of the garments that have been given to you to wear throughout your life.

2. Take your time and write down 10 things that you desire to become.

_____
_____
_____
_____
_____
_____
_____
_____
_____
_____

KNOW THYSELF

Life is full lessons, right? From our inception, we embark upon a life full of learning. From the beginning, our parents begin to teach us the ways of the world. They instruct us on the basic aspects of living. They teach us to walk, talk, eat and many other necessary functions. Then we transition into the stage of our lives where we are instructed through some form of the educational system. It is here where we are given a foundation of processing information. We learn reading, writing, arithmetic and many other subjects. There is even a system of spiritual education that many of us participate in where we are instructed in the supposed ways and requirements of God. In every aspect of our lives, there is some sort of system that has been devised to ensure that we are properly informed except one; there is no established school that teaches you to Know Thyself.

This Ancient Greek Aphorism "Know Thyself," was translated by Plato when he writes Phaedrus and has Socrates say, *"But I have no leisure for them at all; and the reason, my friend, is this: I am not yet able, as the*

Delphic inscription has it, to know myself; so it seems to me ridiculous, when I do not yet know that, to investigate irrelevant things." Socrates was giving his explanation to Phaedrus for why he had no time for Mythology or any other far-flung topics. In essence, what this can mean is that for me to submerse myself in the understanding of every other topic that makes up what we call life apart from the understanding of who I am is futile.

Why is it important to understand and be intimately acquainted with thyself? Your paradigm (or the lenses through which you see life) is critically impactful to your response to life. If you are not keenly aware of who you are, the experiences that you have will probably never yield the lessons and wisdom that they could have otherwise. When I refer to being keenly aware of who you are, I'm not only speaking of knowing your life's purpose but also knowing what it is, that makes you tick. This requires for you to take an honest inventory of yourself. Learn your habits, propensities, likes and dislikes, what makes you mad, what gives you joy. In my opinion, the greatest lesson that you can learn is who you truly are. It will be through this lesson that everything else will flow and where success can be discovered. I believe that as you excavate the grounds of your soul, you will find the Creator. You will begin to understand how you personally relate and communicate with the one that both gives and sustains your life. You will begin to effectively connect in a way that has been developed just for you. You will not be confined to the restrictions, dogmatic requirements and boundaries that have been put in place by others to tell you in what ways you are able to enjoy the essence of who you are. It will not be your testimony, like many others, that you suffer from an identity crisis. Don't be mistaken, there are many people that don't truly know who they are, but have been told who they are.

When you learn, accept and become honest with who you are, you are able to establish the groundwork for personal change or concrete confidence of self that cannot be challenged. This principle translates to every category in life. In spirituality, relationships, careers and overall decision making, you should take your steps from the platform of a healthy understanding of self.

Let it not be mistaken that I am advocating a mindset of total self-sufficiency. Indeed, there is great benefit to be gained from all of the systems that I have mentioned. However, in order for us to get all that we can from this life experience, a true knowledge of thyself must be understood. I implore you to begin/continue to dig into yourself and see what amazing things you will discover. KNOW THYSELF!

BEFORE YOU TURN THE PAGE...

1. Regardless of how advanced your understanding is in different areas, be intentional about taking an internal inventory of who you are.

2. It's okay if you need to come back to his chapter, but write down some of your discoveries about yourself.

_____
_____
_____
_____
_____
_____
_____
_____
_____
_____

A.D. MOORE

TURNING PAGES

Life is the novel of our existence. It is a story that is filled with triumph, struggle, love and even chaos. The pages of life are what form this novel, and it is imperative that you read it in its entirety.

This brings me to several questions.

Why do you hesitate and become afraid to turn the pages? Why do you become content and complacent, failing to read on? Is there a reason to continue? Could this really be the end? Or is there more?

The lack of understanding, the presence of fear, the insecurity created by failure and even the arrogance developed by success are all bookmarks that serve as barriers to the completion of your story. They serve to hold you back, and the only way to overcome them is to turn the page.

Because you won't turn the page, you convince yourself that what you have read up to this point is the sum of your existence. You must understand that this is a novel with many chapters ahead. You may be in a chapter of hurt, confusion, depression or maybe poverty, but the story is not over. Turn the page.

The presence of fear can be a debilitating force. You fear what will happen when you turn the page. But fear is not yours. Fear is a spirit that you don't have. Fear is an influence and fear is a distraction. Don't fear that the next chapter of life will be the same. Don't fear that the pages will continue to read as they always have. The crippling nature of fear will cause you to doubt your God-given ability to overcome, to progress, to dominate. William Ernest Henley, the writer of Invictus, stated:

Beyond this place of wrath and tears
Looms but the Horror of the shade,
and yet the menace of the years
Finds, and shall find, me unafraid.

It matters not how strait the gate,
How charged with punishments the scroll.
I am the master of my fate:
I am the captain of my soul.

You must determine to make fear subject to you. You must take charge and authority over your soul and turn the page.

Your novel has been filled with many different turns of events. Your novel has many pages of victory, happiness, and success, but the pages that you choose to highlight are the pages with paragraphs of failure. Your life has been filled with more abundance than it has lacked. The breath of life is flowing through your brilliantly created body, you may have been blessed to create beautiful and healthy children, and the list goes on and on. You are not your failures. You are not your weaknesses. You are not the opinion of others. Belief in these ideas of you has produced insecurity, but rest assured and be secure in the fact that there is more to your story. Turn the page.

Remember the chapter of your life when you felt that you were on top of the world? Everything was clicking. You felt a sense of importance; you were in a place of social prominence. You comfortably rested in a place of economic stability and life was just good. I mean this is what life is supposed to be like, correct? However, life indeed happened to you just as it has to others and now your life may read differently. Life may be uncomfortable now, and it may be seemingly impossible to tolerate. You may have chosen to continue re-reading the great chapters of your story, but you fail to read on. You bask in the glow of your state championship, election to prom queen, the chiseled body you once had or the people you once dated. Your fear that you can never be greater has you continually reading those chapters of your life in order to experience a sense of security and comfort. Remember that there are many more chapters in your life. There is more greatness yet to be discovered in your novel. The mere fact that success has been yours before convinces me that success is now dormant inside of you, awaiting its resurrection.

Life is the novel of our existence. It is a story that is filled with triumph, struggle, love and even chaos. The pages of life are what form this novel, and it is imperative that you read it in its entirety.

You and I must continue to move forward. Our story is one that has been completed already. Your life has been written, and the Author knows the end from the beginning. With the accomplishments as well as the failures, we must continue to read on. Bookmarks simply delay the triumphant climax and conclusion that is to come. Read on, my friend. Read on and continue turning the pages.

BEFORE YOU TURN THE PAGE...

1. Honestly, answer the questions in this chapter and then choose to move past every success and perceived failure to the next chapter of your life.

_____
_____
_____
_____
_____
_____
_____
_____
_____
_____
_____
_____
_____
_____
_____
_____
_____
_____
_____

THE ART OF DISSOLUTION

I can imagine that some may be confused by the title of this piece; "The Art of Dissolution." So, let's first consider the title in order to set the stage for today's discussion.

Art: The principles or methods governing any craft. Other words that can be used to describe this are a craft, technique, method, way, fine points, subtleties.

Dissolution: 1. the undoing or breaking of a bond, tie, union, partnership, etc. 2. A bringing or coming to an end, disintegration, decay, termination.

There indeed is an art to the act of dissolution. Whether it is an unexpected or welcomed occurrence, we all have or will experience some form of the breaking of a tie or union. How these moments in life are managed will quite often determine how future bonds are initiated and whether or not they are successful.

Most of us (to include myself) can personally attest to the pain, frustration, confusion, intimidation and especially fear that one can experience when someone/thing that they have loved, cared for and invested in begins to slowly or rapidly die and decay. It is in this process that we must carefully begin to consider the steps we take or the methods we use in order to refrain from remaining in a constant state of dissolution. Those that do not carefully and intentionally tread through these moments oftentimes continue to experience separation and disunity within their relationships and never move into the type of relationships that produce life, prosperity, and perpetual joy. We have the responsibility of managing our hearts especially when we are not responsible for the pain and disrespect that may have been inflicted. What we experience in life is real and sometimes beyond our control, but our response to it is always a choice. Your heart is yours to govern and yours to protect. The Word encourages us with these words, *"Keep your heart with all diligence, for out of it flows the issues of life."* (Proverbs 4:23).

The Issue of the Heart

There is a good reason why we are strongly admonished throughout scripture to be mindful of the condition of our hearts. The heart, both naturally and spiritually, is the most important organ. Your heart makes up the person you call "Me." It is the center of your being and is composed of your mind, will and your emotions. How you respond to life, is a direct result of the condition of your heart. How you view life in your mind, is a result of what you have allowed to shape your thinking. How you govern your decisions or will is a result of your thinking. How you feel about certain things is a result of how you think and the decisions you make. When you experience dissolution, it is a very critical time to begin paying attention to the condition of your heart. During this type of process, there can be many things that attempt to shape your thinking in a negative manner. If you are going through the end of a romantic relationship or marriage, you may begin to think or yourself as damaged goods, that no one else will ever want you or maybe that in order to not be lonely that you must lower your standards. Because of this type of thinking, you may start to make decisions that you would not ordinarily make. A man may begin to live in a less than honorable way, or a woman may begin to seek after multiple men instead of allowing the right man to find her as the valuable prize that she is. A man or woman can become bitter and angry. They can feel a sense of resentment or maybe even depression.

At this point, the heart has undergone a full-scale attack. It has been bombarded with an array of untruths, and if it is not aggressively addressed, it will begin to form the person you call "Me." You will become one that thinks less of yourself than you really are, your decisions will begin to lack wisdom, but you will blame everyone else for the way you are.

Truth & Solutions

The only key to overcoming the attack of untruth is to have an understanding of the truth. It is reasonable for us to believe that life will cause us to experience some form of dissolution, but that is the very moment that you have to be sure to guard your heart and counter attack if need be. Regardless of the circumstances of the break, you must remember who you are and who you were meant to be. Men, remind yourself that you are a man of integrity, a man of honor and a man that has been given everything that is needed pertaining to life and Godliness. Women, remind yourselves that you are precious and valuable. Remind yourself that you are a woman of virtue, a woman full of beauty and a woman that is deserving of being cared for and protected.

This is the Art of Dissolution. It is the intentional caring and guarding of your heart. It is the ability to identify the falsehoods that try to shape "Me" and countering with Truth. Again, what we experience in life is real and sometimes beyond our control, but our response to it is always a choice. Learn to guard your heart. Go to whatever lengths are needed to make your heart healthy. Talk to, read and listen to whatever is going to help you become the best "Me" you can be.

BEFORE YOU TURN THE PAGE...

1. What is the current condition of your heart as it relates to relationships that have or appear to be dissolving?

2. Make a choice to avoid carrying the weight of that relationship(s) into other interactions with people.

_____
_____
_____
_____
_____
_____
_____
_____
_____
_____
_____
_____
_____
_____
_____
_____

PROFITABLE PAIN

One of the greatest sounds that I've ever heard was that of my heart breaking. It wasn't always that way. In fact, it used to be the blood-curdling sound that I feared, and yet it seemed to inevitably come. With her, I lived what seemed to be moments of true bliss. I often would fearlessly, yet unwisely sprint to the edge of the cliff and with such grace, I would leap away from the security of the ground beneath me. In that moment, I felt so free. In that moment, I possessed no worries. In that moment, I knew love. Such an amazing feeling it was to be suspended in the air; to not be subject to the downward pull of gravity. I was soaring toward what I believed would be a lifetime of joy. As I happily soared, I could feel the cool and calming breeze against my face. I looked to the horizon before me where I saw the wonderful experiences that awaited me. Suddenly, the calm breeze was replaced with a rushing wind, and the ground beneath me began to aggressively pull me closer. As I rapidly approached the earth, I saw that I was following my heart that was plummeting to the ground in front of me; the same heart that I followed when I decided to leap. It was almost unbearable for me to attempt to process the fear, disappointment, and the confusion that I experienced as they each battled for control within me. But, the fact that I struggled with the most was the fact that I had been here before.

Unfortunately, this was a familiar place for me. She promised to lift my wings. I was lead to believe that her love was real this time. So many times our conversations were short-lived and full of nothing, but to me, they were everything. The fantasy of her was my life, and the reality, my nightmare. If I could just hold on a while longer, she'd reciprocate my love. If I just believe really hard and meet her needs, then I could change her will. I wanted to be her picture of love, but somehow along the way, I forgot to love myself.

Have you ever been so overtaken by your ability to love someone, that you subject yourself to the type of treatment that is clearly not a demonstration of love toward you? Did you ever think that your capacity to love, inclusive of long suffering, the ability to overlook wrongdoing and kindness would ever produce heartache and devastation? In this cycle, it was as if I was constantly intoxicated, causing me to lose my equilibrium and misperceive reality. What I believed to be another great opportunity to get it right this time, was really nothing more than another moment in my journey, designed to develop greater character and preparation for true and meaningful companionship. I know that many of you know this pain. For some of you, this cycle is your life. This cycle is your comfort zone. Believe it or not, this is all to your benefit if you allow it. I'm not subscribing to the saying, "No pain, no gain," but I am saying that where there is pain, there can be great gain.

    I had to learn that this pain that I was consistently having, and maybe even putting myself through, was there to help me formulate the ideas of what I really desired. Knowing the inconsistency made me yearn for consistency. The lack of her touch, increased my desire to be caressed. The absence of quality time established the need for me to connect and share. Through this process, I was learning myself. I was learning what it is that I need. I was learning the ways that I interpret love. This real life lesson was schooling me in the most effective way, but then it was my responsibility to make sure that I only allowed what was going to be beneficial to me from that point.

    I had to decide that the cycle was over. I chose to embrace the lessons. I decided that I did not want to continue to leap, just to rapidly hit rock bottom. I want to take the power of my love and join it with the love of a woman, lift each other and soar together. Remember that weak is the love of someone that cares for others but doesn't care for themselves.

BEFORE YOU TURN THE PAGE...

1. You have to make the decision to bring an end to any cycle(s) that consistently causes you pain. More importantly, you must identify how it can make you stronger and teach you about yourself.

2. In your relationships, ask yourself if you love that person more than you love yourself. If you do, how is it working for you?

_____
_____
_____
_____
_____
_____
_____
_____
_____
_____
_____
_____
_____
_____
_____
_____

A.D. MOORE

CHEATERS

I have cheated on several occasions. To be honest, I started cheating as an adolescent, and I have to admit that some of those occurrences were at the least pleasurable. There was Denise, Claudia, Emily, the three Michelle's, Jennifer and don't forget Sandra (of course these are fake names.). I cheated with these women at different points in my life and some at the same time. I guess it was the excitement of it all. Some provided a sense of sensuality that I had never experienced, others nurtured me almost as good as my own mother, and some were just so much fun to be around. As much as I was able to draw value from each of the women that I encountered, I had to come to the realization that regardless of the pleasure that I was experiencing; I was indeed cheating.

I was withholding the greatest form of love; unconditional love. I was sacrificing valuable time that would never be returned to me. I gave critical energy that could have been used to build and repair. I opened up my heart and mind to ones that didn't have the capacity to care for or appreciate me. I foolishly repeated a cycle that I ignorantly believed would eventually produce satisfactory results. Yes, I know that it was my fault, but I'm sure that you can relate because rumor has it that you have been a cheater just like me! Yes, you! Just like me, I am almost positive that you are or have been just as guilty as I have of cheating on YOURSELF!

This isn't about cheating on your boyfriend/girlfriend or husband/wife; this about how we cheat ourselves. One of the definitions of the word "cheat" is to elude or to deprive of something expected. How many times have you deprived yourself of what you should rightfully expect or ran away from exactly what you needed? I discovered that in my search for her that many of the women that I entertained only served as hamster wheels for me. They served as recreation and fun, exercise and they even made me stronger, but there was no forward movement. They did not assist me in the progression of my life, they did not help me to discover how much further I could go in life. They kept me so occupied that I did not realize that I was trapped inside of a cage. I needed a woman that could be my motivation; a woman that would push me to greater depths and heights; a woman to share in life with me. Nevertheless, I continued to cheat myself and go after or accept less than what I deserved. I have voluntarily eluded women that were suitable all because I was immature or afraid. I found myself willing to endure what would never be what I need. I allowed myself to be mistreated, misused and manipulated.

I know that you can find yourself within some or maybe all of my confession. You have cheated yourself and given away some of the most precious moments of your life. You too have given of your time and energy in the hope that your effort would cause you to move forward. You decided to run harder, move faster and think positively, but you always found yourself on that same hamster wheel. Maybe you only thought that it was all their fault, but in actuality, they were only doing what they were capable of.

You are such an incredible creation! You are deserving of love, companionship, happiness and peace. You deserve to exist in the earth with someone that you can form a team/partnership with, but until you realize that you are cheating and encaging yourself, you may never experience that connection. Let us not be so quick to jump on the wheel because of loneliness. Let us not be so quick to jump on the wheel because of obligation. Let us not be so quick to jump on the wheel because of impatience. We can have exactly what we expect and need. Cheating ourselves will no longer be our option.

BEFORE YOU TURN TH PAGE...

1. In what ways have you cheated yourself in your life relationships?

2. Who are the people that are hamster wheels in your life?

3. Write down the reasons why you deserve to have someone that helps you to progress through life.

_____
_____
_____
_____
_____
_____
_____
_____
_____
_____
_____
_____

FINGER LOVE

I find it to be quite fascinating that the simple strokes and movements of a finger can bring so much pleasure to someone. With its simple strokes, it can produce a sense of ecstasy and raw emotion. Men and women alike go to great lengths and have sleepless nights just to experience a brief moment of Finger love. Sadly, there are times when some feel hurt when they realize that they aren't the only one that has been pleasured by the same fingers as they have. Sadly, there are times when some place way more significance than they should in this form of attention. The use of fingers has somehow become the standard of affection. They alone have the ability to forge a relationship and even tear one down. Is it really that powerful or have we created this power in our minds? Come with me for a moment as we explore the impact social media has on our emotional lives.

How did we get to the place in our world where we live for "Likes" and "Follows"? The verbal and physical expression of love, affection, and interest are quickly being replaced with the simple click of a mouse or the double-tap of a phone screen. Somehow people have begun to interpret these actions as a sign of love and affection, and when these actions are directed at others, it's a sign of betrayal and dislike. Many people seem to find validation through others' appreciation of the persona that they've created in social media. It is a place where someone's insecurities are under their control. They can find solace through cropping, filters and camera angles. They, at times, have worked very diligently to create these images of themselves, and they want nothing more than for you to please them with some good ol' finger love. Now, I have to be completely honest about myself as it relates to this. I too, know what is to seek after the attention of others in social media. For me, receiving likes and follows, served as an ego booster. It represented acceptance and inclusion in my life. It served as a temporary remedy in my times of loneliness.

Please understand that I am in no way demonizing anyone that finds joy in participating in any form of social media. It can be very fun, it has brought many people together, and many businesses have been able to thrive because of it. Adversely, some people's response to the things that take place on social media has resulted in destroyed relationships, depression and even death. So, if social media itself can produce both positive and negative results; it means that what it produces and how we respond is up to us. My desire for us all is to find our validation within and with those in our lives that actually matter. Know that regardless of the images that you present, regardless of the number of likes, regardless of the amount of people that follow you and regardless of the amount of people that ignore you all together; you can find your validation and acceptance from within. You are the greatest creation that ever was or will be. Some will recognize it and some won't. Some will express to you how wonderful you are, and some will say the opposite. Let it never be said that the finger love that others give you supersedes the love that you give to yourself. Use social media for its purpose, and remember that its purpose is not to let you know who you are. Enjoy your life and have fun sharing it! Let's use it to build each other up. Let's use it to mobilize the masses toward peace and love. Let's use it to keep the bonds of friendship and family alive.

BEFORE YOU TURN THE PAGE...

1. If you are involved in social media, is your profile an accurate representation of who you are, and do you depend on it to build your self-esteem and worth?

___
___
___
___
___
___
___
___
___
___
___
___
___
___
___
___

DEFENSE MECHANISMS

Many of us have developed specific defense mechanisms throughout the course of our lives due to different invasions of our peace of mind and body. We instinctively learn to protect ourselves from any and everything that causes us harm or appears to have the potential to inflict pain on us. This is a natural response, and it is one that should be embraced and even developed. Too often, people allow themselves to become doormats for others to deposit the filth that they carry within their character. Some fail to protect their heart/soul with the type of armor that can withstand the attacks that life and/or others strike against us. Then there are those that have effectively learned to wear the armor and properly defend themselves against the attackers that they have become accustomed to.

A defense mechanism in and of itself is a necessary tool to possess, and without this tool, one could walk in a constant state of vulnerability. However, as much as this may be a necessary tool to develop, it is equally important to realize when it is time to take the armor off.

Picture for a moment the image of a medieval knight. This knight is covered from head to toe in armor that is intended to be impenetrable. His head is covered so that he is able to maintain the faculties of his mind and brain functions. His torso is covered so that his heart and vital organs are able to continue providing life to the rest of the body. His arms and legs are covered so that he is able to stand firm and hold on to the weapons and tools needed for battle. His feet are covered so that he is able to maintain stability and balance in the midst of an attack. Everything that he wears carries with it a positive purpose of protection.

Now, let's picture this same knight as he goes home from a long day of battle to be with his loved ones. He has been bombarded all day by enemies that meant to do him great harm, but he was victorious. He has returned home from his noble duties, but he has refused to remove the armor. I hope that you see the problem with this. In his loved ones there is a need that they have to experience intimacy with him and in order to fulfill this need, they need to have access to every area that he now habitually covers. Unfortunately, this prevents those closest to him from becoming intimately acquainted with him. They need to have access to his mind. It is important for them to know the thoughts of his heart; to be able to draw from the intelligence that he has gained. They need to have access to his heart; to be able to draw life from the innermost parts of his being. The heart is the center of who he is, and they want to become a central part of who he is. They need to have access to his arms and legs; to be able to be carried and embraced, protected and walked with. They need to have access to his feet; to benefit from his ability to dig in and not be moved during their moments of instability. Overall, they need to feel the warmth of his body. They need to experience his humanity and know that he is a man of like passions and like trials. Can you imagine how uncomfortable it would be to be physically intimate with this person or how difficult it would be to hear his voice and look into his eyes? Yet many of us live in this manner. We live a life that is so guarded, so rigid and so inwardly lonely. The ones that you need to draw life from are held at bay by the securely fixed barriers that you are too fearful to remove.

"How do I know when it is safe to lower my guard and remove my armor?" "I have lived a life under attack!" "I have been hurt in so many ways and by so many people." "The last time I let my guard down, I regretted it very much!" These may all be thoughts that immediately arise in your mind. But now that you understand how critical it is for you to allow people in and why your defenses must be lowered; you now must identify whether someone is a friend or foe.

On the one hand, you have grown so accustomed to fighting and defending yourself that you do not allow anyone into the intimate areas of your life. On the other hand, you ignorantly and prematurely remove your armor to later learn that the intention of the one before you is harm. It is vital that you take the necessary time to evaluate the motivation of those you choose to remove your armor for. That which you have to offer is valuable and irreplaceable. It is too precious to allow it to be violated, but so needed that it should not be hidden or withheld.

It's time to do a self-evaluation. How do you live day to day with those closest to you and how do you protect yourself from those without? Remember, defense mechanisms are necessary tools that must be properly developed. There is nothing wrong with them until you consciously or sub-consciously use them to avoid intimacy. How comfortable is it for your loved ones to get close you? ***Maybe it's time to tear the barriers down.***

BEFORE YOU TURN THE PAGE...

1. Think about and write down the ways that your defense mechanisms are manifested?

2. Ask your loved ones if they feel that you are guarded against them.

3. With those in your life that have proven themselves trustworthy, make an intentional effort to start taking off your armor.

_____

_____

_____

_____

_____

_____

_____

_____

_____

_____

_____

_____

_____

_____

NAKED

There is a defining moment in your life and in all of your relationships when you choose to embrace the beauty of your nakedness. It is in this moment that peace is experienced and lasting bonds are made. To be naked is to be totally stripped of everything that serves to cover or hide who you truly are. From the beginning of time, we have been conditioned to seek refuge behind an outer shell: safety inside of a seemingly indestructible suit of armor. Vulnerability is rarely the order of the day and trust in another human being is viewed as one of the great paradoxes of the world. Instead of being naked and unashamed, many are covered and proud of the deceptive garment that they daily wear.

It goes without saying that complete vulnerability is not always the wisest choice. We all have a natural need to protect ourselves because of the environment that we live in. To protect against the hard terrain, we wear suitable shoes. To protect ourselves from the sometimes harsh elements of nature, we wear the appropriate clothing. We also wear certain clothing in order to cover the physical insecurities that many of us have. Because we are so accustomed to covering and or masking our natural bodies, I believe that many of those same methods are implemented in our lives emotionally. To allow yourself to be emotionally vulnerable is one of the great challenges of life. To expose your inner thoughts, pain and insecurities to someone can sometimes seem to be an emotional suicide, but it is the only way to experience true and unconditional love.

How beautiful is a love that is not restricted or limited by conditions; a love that totally embraces the beauty in your state of raw nakedness? It is a love that's patience is evident when your true self provokes restlessness and irritation. It's a love that expresses kindness and keeps no record of the many wrongs that you commit. This love finds joy in every blemish, your every propensity and your every unique challenge. It's a love that can only be demonstrated and expressed to the real YOU.

This is what makes the love of God so significant and powerful. God, who is all-seeing and all-knowing, has created you and can see you in your nakedness. He has abundantly expressed his love to you without measure. When you are in your absolute worst condition, God's love is able to reach into the deep and dark crevices of your existence and embrace you. It's the ultimate unconditional love, so it matters not how much you attempt to cover and hide the blemishes of your life. It is this pure and unadulterated love that loves you in spite of you. Not only does the love of God transcend any level of support and acceptance that exist, but it also serves as the example to us of the level of love that we can experience with one another.

My desire for you is for you to connect with someone with whom you can boldly exist in a state of nakedness. Live in the place where there is no need to mask the truth of who you are. You can accept exactly who you are and comfortably improve upon yourself because someone has already decided to embrace you in spite of you. This is what many relationships are missing, and I believe, for this reason, many relationships fail. All too often, men and women fall in love with the false image that was presented to them just as much as they present a false image. They often commit their lives to one another, but what they really do is say, "I commit to live with you without complete trust, and I promise to only give you the side of me that I have managed to perfect."

With those who deserve it, I encourage you to remove your suit of armor, accept and embrace your nakedness and choose to love unconditionally.

BEFORE YOU TURN THE PAGE...

1. In your relationships, are/will you be willing to be naked before your mate?

2. Do you have to capacity to love someone in spite of the blemishes they may possess?

SKILLFUL INTERCOURSE

There is an intense feeling of euphoria that is experienced when you encounter someone that is skillful in intercourse. The orgasm that is shared transcends the physical world into the spiritual realm where it is best understood. The exchange is so amazing that it causes you to yearn for it constantly. I love to be satisfied with this intercourse when I awake, as I travel through my day and before I retire each night. It has become a necessity in my life, and I make intentional efforts to hone my skills so that I too may be the provider of this feeling. I want to give so intensely that my deposits remain and are able to be enjoyed even in my physical absence. The thoughts of eternally entering someone give me life. The arousal that I will create energizes me to find ways to touch places that only reside in the deep recesses of someone's heart.

Intercourse Defined:

1. Dealings or communication between individuals, groups or countries.

2. Interchange of thoughts, feelings.

I am speaking about how to develop skillful communication; developing the ability to effectively express and interchange your thoughts, desires, and emotions with someone. Through the words of our communication, we can figuratively place our hearts inside of others. We can represent the spark that ignites the fire needed to be inspired. We can cause them to experience a lasting euphoria that cannot be rivaled. Indeed, words are powerful.

Let us use our words to promote love, joy, and peace. Use your words to build esteem and use your words to tear down insecurity, fear, and doubt. Through your words, you can shine light into dark places. Through your words, you can tear down the Jericho like walls that many have erected around their hearts and minds. Through your words, you can cause her rivers to flow or his blood to surge. Enjoy the freedom that is experienced when you have a beautiful interchange of thoughts and feelings. Discover how blissful it is to see someone take your very heart and decide to carry it with them.
Embrace the feeling that you have when all you want to do is share moments giving each other

deep and intentional words. Let us find the pleasure that is available to us by becoming skillful in the expression of our hearts through words.

    Spread your hearts open and allow love to come in.

BEFORE YOU TURN THE PAGE...

1. Practice compliments

   Give unasked for praise for an action or some quality you genuinely admire in another person. Give it without reservation or an expectation attached.

   _____
   _____
   _____
   _____
   _____
   _____
   _____
   _____
   _____
   _____
   _____
   _____
   _____
   _____

TOUCH YOURSELF

Several times today, I touched myself! It was the most exhilarating experience of personal pleasure that I've ever enjoyed. I knew exactly what I needed. I grabbed it and began to gently, aggressively and proficiently massage the most sensitive areas, culminating in the most euphoric explosion of absolute bliss and satisfaction. I discovered that there was no person that had the ability to please me in this fashion, and I took full responsibility for this feeling, never to relinquish this task to another again. There were times when I would allow someone to participate as I touched myself. They would come along and yield to my needs and even my instructions to ensure that I had the most pleasure. Oh my God! To know that I was being blessed with this incredible and overwhelming stimulation was so amazing, but what was even more mind-blowing was the thought that when they stopped participating, that my bliss would not end!

    I write this as a devout advocate of this practice. You absolutely have to take full responsibility for this experience. I even recommend that you even invite someone to enjoy touching you at the same time you pleasure yourself, but not until you first master this art of self-gratification.

Before you continue to think of this as an erotic expose' of my freaky escapades, let's take a deeper look into what I said. This concept of touching yourself is not sexual in nature. It is the act of making yourself happy. In this act, I explore the intricate details my being. I endeavor to discover the intimate parts of who I am, and in essence, I grab those parts of my heart and/or mind and I massage them in whatever way is needed to make sure that I feel good. This is the art of taking full responsibility for creating an existence of happiness. It is the understanding that it feels so wonderful when someone else can come and add to my happiness, but also the wisdom to not make anyone else assume this role because you know that all they can really do is add a bonus to your amazing moment.

The failure to both observe and practice this is one of the main reasons for unhealthy relationships and miserable cycles. Choosing not to assume the primary role in the creation of your happiness is the equivalent of going to a bookie and completely relying on them to tell you where and how you should bet your money. You would naturally expect them to advise you in a way that is only beneficial to them. When you place your well-being in the care of others, you decide to gamble with your heart with an unrealistic sense of hope.

This job is yours alone. You have to take charge over what makes you happy. You have to take the time to touch yourself and discover the areas of your life that bring you pleasure. You are the only one that is capable of accomplishing this task because you are the one that knows exactly what is needed. It is faulty thinking that you need someone to complete you, you just need to find someone that will love you or that you need to find your better half. Absolutely everything that you need can be found within. The decision to bring another person into your life shouldn't be to fill a void but to add to your current state of happiness. This is just like the person that joins you in an already wonderful experience. If you have taken responsibility for the state of your happiness, and you have also found someone to be your bonus, but they leave; you don't sense that a void has been created and you don't feel a deficit of love and happiness. The only thing that you have lost is the added pleasure, which is not the best experience, but you avoid the depression and other negative challenges that people go through. When you have chosen to depend on others, and they leave, you will scramble to fill that void with someone else that you also allow to have full charge of your well-being. You find yourself in a miserable cycle wondering how come there isn't anyone that can complete you, but what you don't realize is that they were never able to and that you are the one that created this void.

Your search for happiness in relationships begins with you. It begins with you exploring the wonders of who you really are. It is refusing to deprive yourself of the pleasures that have always been available to you, even in your times of loneliness. Take sole responsibility for your love and happiness, and let go of the task that others have given you to complete them and be the sole provider of their well-being. As you decide to add others to your life, only allow those that are a benefit to it. They are meant to share in your world, not create it. Add those who have also mastered this art of self-gratification, and simply want you to help you to feel even better.

The joy and liberation that awaits you is possibly unlike you ever imagined. I challenge you to embark on the incredible journey of self-love and happiness. Each day, enjoy touching yourself, touching each other and together witnessing the most powerful explosion of purpose, passion, and bliss.

BEFORE YOU TURN THE PAGE...

1. Identify Your Strengths: We all have a set of core strengths that can serve as a foundation for building happiness in life. By identifying and claiming your strengths (as opposed to just obsessing about your wants and weaknesses), you'll experience more success and satisfaction in your work, activities, and relationships.

_____

_____

_____

_____

_____

_____

_____

_____

_____

_____

_____

_____

HER BLESSED ASSURANCE

I have seen many injustices under the sun, but possibly none greater than the destruction and demotion of the black woman. For centuries, there has been a very effective campaign in motion that is designed to pervert the world's image, and even worse, the self-image of the greatest woman to ever occupy the earth. She has lost her importance, her value plummets daily, and she has forgotten (or maybe never knew) who she really is. She realizes not that she derives from that which at a time was celebrated, protected and even worshipped. She realizes not that she is a descendant of the original woman; the woman that was the first of all antiquity. She realizes not that her originality is tainted when she begins to adopt the image of that which is not like her. The world tells her to be anyone except who she is. It tells her that her physical image from head to toe is not acceptable; that she can't succeed in life or that she can't find love unless she changes. My sisters, these are merely a few of the tactics that have been put in place to destroy you but fret not, for there is a Blessed Assurance.

You are Blessed!

There is absolutely none like you in the earth. You have been divinely and supremely favored by the Almighty Creator. You are without question, God's greatest creation; a model that was carefully hand-crafted to display God's glory. From the twist of your hair, the hue of your skin and to the magnificent curves of your body; you serve as the model and desire for others.

Your hair sits upon your head as a crown fit for a queen. Did you know that the twist of your hair mimics the spiraling of the universe, the plants as they emerge through the soil and the blood as it travels through the veins? In other words, your beautiful so-called nappy hair is a representation of life and growth. Think about how amazing your hair really is. It can be manipulated to take on many different forms. You can make your hair look like that of just about any race of people, but no other race can effectively make their hair look like yours.

"The black skin is not a badge of shame, but rather a glorious symbol of national greatness." –Marcus Garvey

Oh, how beautiful you are! Your skin is an object of great jealousy. Industries, products, and professions have been created to attempt to duplicate the hue of your outer shell. Women all over the globe, labor in the sun and religiously give monetarily to achieve this symbol of greatness. The strength of your skin allows you to endure the changing climates and with slow motion, it ages and maintains its amazing glow. Your skin is the purest image of the earth from which you came. As the dark earth has given birth to all that we know naturally, so you have given birth to all mankind. Sister, wear your skin as the garment of greatness that it is.

As a child (even as an adult honestly), I have always found great pleasure when I had the opportunity to ride, run or even roll down the curves of the ground. It served as a form of recreation and fun. When I wanted to condition my body, I would often traverse similar hills in order to develop the muscles of my legs and/or arms. I guess it is no surprise as to why I enjoy the curves of a beautiful black woman. Oh my God! You are so incredible! Every shape and every size is a demonstration or display of the handy work of a divine artist. From the fullness of your lips to the wideness of your hips, I experience joy and security. Again, many women have gone to great and dangerous lengths in a desperate effort to possess what you were blessed with.

Sista, I could go on and on about God's wonderful creation that is you, but I want to encourage you to go on and on about yourself. Stand amongst the masses with pride. Fully understand that you are divinely favored by God. Walk this earth that you built with unmatched self-esteem and be confident being you. You are my model and desire. You gave me life, you nurtured me, and you daily sustain me. You represent life, strength, and passion. The design of your being says that God is love. The world wants you, so look in the mirror and start wanting yourself.

BEFORE YOU TURN THE PAGE...

1. Look in the mirror and love on yourself! Say I love you to your reflection 3x a day. The more you do this, the more you will fall in love with yourself.

_____
_____
_____
_____
_____
_____
_____
_____
_____
_____
_____
_____
_____
_____
_____

PROVIDENCE

Have you ever taken a moment to consider the orchestration of events in your life? Does it cause you to ask questions like: Why does this person keep coming in and out of my life? Why did I meet them at this seemingly inopportune time? Why did our relationship not survive as I expected it to? Or how come I can't be with them right now? Well, it may be beneficial for you to take the time to try to understand the divine providence of God. As you understand this concept, I believe that it will bring comfort to your heart. The pain, frustration, and confusion can be relieved.

Providence has to do with God, with all power, directing the universe and the affairs of humankind with wisdom through love. This doesn't mean that we are simply puppets being strung along through life by some big being in the sky, but it does suggest that God, being all-knowing and seeing, can see the end from the beginning and knows how to masterfully move heaven and earth to ensure your success. The key is to work with God and the universe in order to move in graceful concert together. In my experience, there are tremendous lessons that can be learned from understanding how the Creator conducts the affairs of creation. One of the most effective ways to teach the idea of providence is through a look at natural parenthood. Any good parent desires the continual success of their child. As a parent and adult, you have a broader outlook on life than your child does. You have, in many cases, experienced most of what your child will. Your child doesn't completely understand why they can't do certain things or why they must do others. They live their lives in the moment and through emotion. All they know is how something makes them feel and what they want to do. They rarely consider the lessons, character or wisdom that you are attempting to develop in them. We, as adults, are not all that different. Sure, we have much more understanding of life than your average child; sure we have forethought and plans for life, but we can easily get caught up in the moments and emotions of our lives. We very often don't understand why some things are the way they are. Much like children, we have our version of temper tantrums when life does not go our way. I want to propose to you that if you remember that our God is full of providence and love for you and that these attributes of God are strictly in your favor, you can be at peace.

I guess what I am attempting to do is help you develop or maintain a heart of optimism. You must be able to see the benefit of all your circumstances in life. I would have never thought that I would be in my 30's as a divorced parent. My vision for the path of my life was very different. I was to be, in my opinion, on a different course. I, like many of you, would never write trial, depression, struggle, loneliness or heartache into the story of my life. Until, recently in my life, I didn't realize that it was these painful events that I experienced that served as catalysts to develop me into the man that I am. It was through my trials that I saw God as my advocate. It was through my depression that I began to know what peace really felt like. It was through my struggles that I learned how much strength I possessed. It was through my loneliness that I learned to love myself. It was in the midst of my heartache that I finally knew what love felt like. I'm sure that your story is similar to mine. Yours has been full of things that you would have never volunteered for, but it has served to make you the person that you are today.

Please understand that the reality of life is that there is more that you will experience in this life that you did not request, and sometimes you and I need reminders that God is wise and full of providence. We must sometimes fight to see the benefit that we experience through unfortunate circumstances. It is our choice of how we are to respond to life. There will be times when you feel overwhelmed, and there will be times when you feel as though you failed, but remember that the Creator cares for the creation and your positive response to life's troubles can allow your troubles to become triumphs!

BEFORE YOU TURN THE PAGE...

1. Think About an unfavorable outcome that happened in your life.

2. How did God show Providence?

3. What was the lesson in the outcome?

LET GO AND LET YOU

In most of my writing, you may notice that I often refer to purpose. The word "purpose" speaks of that which naturally occurs for you. It describes the parts of you that beautifully flow in concert with who you truly are. Whether we're talking about life, professional or romantic purpose, it has to do with something flowing effortlessly. When our purpose is discovered, we can have so much joy and peace because it is these things that require the least amount of human effort. It's something that has a lesser amount of fatigue as you pursue it because its connection with you is a divine connection. This is what our hearts should yearn for. Seek after those things that bring you inner peace; those things that make you feel happy; those things that make you feel like you.

Many times we unknowingly, through our human effort, restrict or add resistance to this natural flow. I believe that this happens because of our adherence to the societal norms or because we think that we have to work for everything that is good in our lives, but what's yours is yours, and you have every right to have it. In our world, we are celebrated for how hard we work toward things. Because of this, we have been conditioned to believe that pain and discomfort are methods of achieving your goals. We then tell ourselves that if something seems to come easily, that it is surely temporary. Phrases such as "No pain, no gain" have become a part of life's motto, yet we never adjust to the fact that sometimes we seem to experience more pain than gain. I believe that when you learn to let go, you can allow yourself to become the real you. You can begin to move toward the goals and ambitions that you have, and you can begin to attract the divine connections that you were meant to.

There are two illustrations that I want to give you that can help you to visualize the benefits of letting go.

River Flow: Imagine that you are in a canoe which will represent your life, and your canoe is in a river which will represent the world that you live in. In this river, your goal is to achieve all that it has to offer you. You are trying to get to that which is yours (purpose). Just like with any river, there is a current or direction in which this river flows. You have no ability to change the natural current of this river. It is what it is. If you are like most, you will use the strength that you have to paddle upstream and against the current of this river. Depending on your strength, you may be able to travel a far distance. You will possibly enjoy the scenery as you travel up this river, and undoubtedly, you will have pleasant moments. Initially, it seems that you are making progress and that you are reaching your purpose, but there comes a time when your strength starts to dwindle, your travel begins to slow, and it's not as fun anymore. Now, it starts to become work. You may solicit the help of others and begin to travel farther, but eventually, their strength gives out, and now you have the same dilemma. You tried as hard as you could, but you failed to understand something so critical; the river was attempting to take you exactly where you wanted to go all along. The current of this river is your built in transportation. It wants nothing more than to carry you to that place of purpose, destiny, and abundance. If you would simply let go; release the oars and allow it to take you there regardless of your human intervention. Think of how much energy you can save as you allow the current to take you along at the exact pace that you need to travel. You get to enjoy watching everything that is yours be revealed to you in its time. Imagine laying back while coasting down the river with the assurance that you are exactly where you need to be.

Magnetic Attraction: I can remember as a child, playing with magnets. I was fascinated by how I could place them close to each other and watch them snap together. What was even more amazing to me was when I attempted to put two magnets together, and they refused to connect. No matter how hard I tried, I could not remove the invisible force that was constantly driving a wedge between the two. As I would bring one magnet close to the next, you could literally feel the barrier. Sometimes, I would force the two together just to see if I could, but as soon as I released the pressure, they rapidly separated. For whatever reason, they were simply not meant to connect. Likewise, there are those that you attract and even those that you may repel. Have you ever thought about someone that is absolutely drawn to you and you to them? There is a magnetic force that seems to pull you close to each other and then when you are close; Snap! Instant connection! It's such a beautiful thing because it isn't something that is manufactured, it is all natural. Oh, how amazing it is to draw in the same person that is drawing you. The need to create thoughts and emotions doesn't exist, and true connection can take place. However, there is another reality that many experience. It is the relationship some have where they sense and feel an invisible barrier between themselves and the other, and connection between the two of them can only happen through force, much like when I would forcefully hold the two magnets together. These people know that if they let up on the pressure that an abrupt separation will surely take place, but they fail to accept that true and natural connection may never happen with that person. At some point, the strength to hold this type of relationship together starts to fail. They're exhausted from all the work, they aren't enjoying themselves, and inner peace is not theirs. Sometimes you have to let go. My desire is that we would truly seek after the purpose that is stubbornly attached to our hearts. We have to responsibly let go of all of the unnecessary work. Some of us are trying too hard to get to the wrong place. Allow the river to flow in your lives and position yourselves to attract what/who you desire.

BEFORE YOU TURN THE PAGE...

1. Take a moment to identify the ways in which you are attempting to force things to happen in your life.

2. Are you expending too much energy to create open doors or relationships?

3. You can achieve your dreams, and the universe wants nothing more than to give it to you.

_____
_____
_____
_____
_____
_____
_____
_____
_____
_____
_____
_____
_____
_____

THE CALL

Why is it that one of the most difficult decisions to make is the one that embodies your purpose? Inside of you all is the sometimes gentle, sometimes forceful and always constant voice that beckons you towards what gives your life validity and meaning. It calls you to itself regardless of your plans, and it confidently remains in place knowing that it is only in that place that you will find peace. This call is like water that rests inside of the teapot of your existence. It is constantly trying to reach its boiling point, and it whistles to indicate to you that it is yearning to overflow and be poured out of you. It says to you, "I am uncomfortable in this place." It says, "I have a burning desire to be released into the atmosphere for all the earth to see and experience me."

This voice is never silenced, but through life's circumstances, we muffle this constant voice much like pouring cold or lukewarm water into an already boiling pot of water. Why do we choose to take a deaf ear to the whistle of purpose? Why are we afraid to allow the infilling of the creator to become an outpouring of His life and virtue?

We fail to realize that the call is a natural part of who we are and oftentimes we attempt to run from something that is virtually anatomically connected to us. God, in His faithfulness, has given us a way of escape from every evil influence, from all temptation and immorality. He shows us how to navigate the waters of life and gives us the clear path toward him. But, when we are attempting to run or navigate our way from God, who is there to assist us? God will not aid you in running away from who He has created you to be. For God to help you avoid the person that He designed you to be would be as though He is confessing that you were inadequately designed and that He has ultimately made a mistake. The truth is that you and I have been fearfully and wonderfully made. You have been thoroughly equipped and fitted with life-giving and altering capacity. You have been built with purpose and destiny that can only be operated by an affirmative answer to the call.

You must listen to the echoing call of purpose inside of you. You must allow the virtue of our Creator to continue to fill you. You must allow God to shape and mold you into a vessel of truth, and most importantly you must allow all of that purpose to overflow out of you into the earth. You have to hear and respond to the call and determine within yourself that you will die empty. What does it mean to die empty? To die empty is to leave this natural existence having given all that God has given you. You have to pour out! The dreams and visions that you know you have cannot leave this earth with you. Your responsibility is to release every drop of life that is within you. You have to overcome your fears and selfishness and commit to the giving of yourself to others. Understand that the call is not a call that is designed to simply impact and improve your life. The call is for you to impact others and find your peace and prosperity in the process.

God cannot and will not aid you in denying your created purpose. The choice is yours. Hear the call! Let's pour out!

BEFORE YOU TURN THE PAGE...

1. Will you continue to ignore the whistle of purpose inside of you?

2. Will you continue to allow the circumstance of life to prevent God's purpose from reaching its boiling point within?

3. Will you refuse to pour out for the world to see?

4. Will you continue in your futile effort of running away from what is the essential part of who you are?

5. Will you choose to die full of purpose or will you leave this earth empty?

_____

_____

_____

_____

_____

_____

_____

_____

_____

_____

ADORN

It was a cold November day, and he was wandering through the forest. It was at times like this where he felt closest to the Creator. He would spend his time taking in all God's wonders and communing with the non-physical version of himself. Everywhere he looked, he saw love. He noticed how the sun expressed its love by providing light in the darkness, warmth in the cold and life to all things. He noticed the clouds. He saw how they expressed their love by releasing cleansing waters that bring refreshment. They provided his warm body with a cooling shade, and they exercised his imagination as he could identify many different shapes and figures within their various forms. What he enjoyed the most were the trees. In the trees, he could feel love intensely radiating from the roots to the tips of the highest leaves. The love of the trees is a special love to him. They amorously gave him love in so many ways. They were directly connected to the earth and grounded in strength. They gave him shelter, a place to hide and they even provided nourishment to his body.

With each calculated step, he grounded himself to the earth with his bare feet as he enjoyed the scenery. As he traversed the land, like a moth to a flame, he was drawn to a single tree. Wonderful feelings of joy and peace overcame him. He was instantly taken back to moments of his childhood when he would sit in front of similar trees at home in late December. He sat at the foot of this tree in pure adoration. He was in amazement of its beauty and strength. He wanted to enjoy it at home as he did when he was a child, but there was no way that he could bring himself to cut it down; he had to let it live. This was a special tree that deserved special honor, and he wanted to give it what it was due.

Full of excitement, he rushed back to the city to make preparations. Each plan was carefully thought out as he prepared to adorn this tree that had done so much for him. After everything had been selected, he hurried back to the forest. Reconnecting himself to the earth again, he began to anxiously walk back to the tree. He had no difficulty finding it again because it was if it were beckoning him to itself.

Standing before it, he offered his gratitude, and he started to adorn it. He began at the base of the tree by digging shallow paths all around it to allow water to flow to it. He then started wrapping a string of pearls from the trunk up to the top. He strategically placed mirror-like ornaments around the tree which allowed him to see his reflection as he admired it. Next, he gently applied natural oils all over it, giving it a sweet and intoxicating fragrance. Finally, he placed a beautiful reflective ring at the top which reflected the sun's glory and signified the eternal connection that they shared with each other. Having completed his adornment of the tree, he stood back and basked in its glory. He felt a sense of accomplishment and gratitude. He felt a mutual love.

This is a story of a man's love for his woman. It's about a man that was connected to God and learned to identify love in all that exist. As he traveled through his life, he encountered so many women, much like one would trees in a forest. Among all of the women, there was one that had a magnetic energy that intensely drew him to her. She was steeped in beauty and grounded in strength, and before meeting him, she had her own connection with God, and she was living her own life. He had no desire to cut her off and become her source of life; he had to let her live. The love that she gave him was such a special love. In her, he found shelter. She was his safe place, and with her, he felt covered and secure. She was his hiding place. In her, he was able to escape the negativity and stresses of the world. She also nourished him. The healthy love that she fed him was chock full of nutrients that kept his heart full and satisfied.

Having finally been drawn to the one, he made preparations for her, and he began to adorn her. He created an environment for her where love and life would always flow to her, and where she never senses a drought or absence of it. The string of pearls symbolized how from her foundation, she was clothed in innocence, purity, and wisdom. Like the mirrored ornaments, when he looked at her, he could see his reflection, reminding him to always treat her as though it were himself. He appreciated the figurative fragrance that emanated from her and beckoned him into her presence. The reflective ring symbolized how she reflected the glory of God and his desire to be eternally connected to her.

Very often, he would stand back and enjoy her glory. As he looked upon her, he would be overcome with gratitude and adoration for her. She helped to give him life, and he was honored to add to hers.

BEFORE YOU TURN THE PAGE...

You are this woman! As you are right now, you are worthy of adoration and praise. You deserve to be adorned and honored by someone, and this is what you should expect. I am so grateful for all that you represent. You make our world go around, and you sustain us daily. This level of adoration starts with you! You must begin/continue to view yourself in this manner. Keep yourself grounded and connected, and never allow anyone to detach you from your Source. Love, peace, and purpose are yours for the taking. Go look in the mirror and find it.

With all my love,

A.D.

ABOUT THE AUTHOR

A.D. Moore is the product of a loving, strong and generous single woman who laid the foundation for him to become an inspiration and leader to many. He found ways to use the challenges that life gives to create opportunities for both personal and professional development. He uses the power of the written and spoken word to create an environment for positive change that enables people to awaken to the greatness that is within us all.

A.D. firmly believes that one of the most effective ways to influence someone to the place of lasting change is through transparency and practical tools. He also believes that if he can serve as a mirror to his readers and listeners that they will be able to take inventory of themselves and ultimately improve their lives overall.

As an Author and writer, A.D. has attained a level of understanding that has produced wisdom beyond his years as it relates to human interaction and relationships.

A.D. is the proud father of two beautiful children.

www.ingramcontent.com/pod-product-compliance
Lightning Source LLC
LaVergne TN
LVHW051506070426
835507LV00022B/2946